The Bear, the Trout, and the Moose

Richard A. Jensen

D1240852

VANTAGE PRESS
New York

Published by Vantage Press, Inc.
419 Park Ave. South, New York, NY 10016

Manufactured in the United States of America
ISBN: 978-0-533-15965-9

Library of Congress Catalog Card No: 2007909652

0 9 8 7 6 5 4 3 2 1

To my wife and children

Contents

Author's Note

Every book has a purpose.

My real reason for writing this book is an attempt to address the age-old question: "Why are we here?" The answer is actually quite simple: I say, "We are all *here* because we are not all *there*."

Intrigued? Well then, sit down, pour yourself a cup of coffee, and let me explain.

It is a wonderful thing to wake up next to a lake. The wind is usually calm, so the only sounds you will hear are the chattering of early-birds, winged and otherwise. (I have my coffee now, so let's continue.)

There are no bears, trout or moose at this lake. It is a prairie lake, which means it formed from the runoff of farmland, and is marginally deeper than ten feet. It gets very green in mid-Summer (now) due to algae, supported from phosphates from agriculture and other sources. Still, it is the lake I wake up to on many weekends.

When I got up this morning, I looked down at the rug at my feet, and saw a bear, a trout and a moose. This may seem like a cop-out when choosing the title for a book, except that the people who design rugs must know what the people who buy rugs like; I did buy this rug, after all.

I am happier at this place than at any other place on this earth. I have been to a few places in my life, but not that many.

I was born and raised on a farm in central South Dakota, but left to move to the big city (Sioux Falls) and have watched it grow from a sleepy prairie town to a frantic prairie town. I have a home in Sioux Falls, but like the lake as a place to reshape my thoughts, and reassess my priorities.

I am a physician, but my passion is flying. I learned to fly before I became a doctor, which means I fell in love with flying before I had the means to enjoy it. I shaped my practice to utilize my flying, which is not difficult in South Dakota, being a sparsely-populated, rural state.

I realize as I sit here, that there are many lessons in our lives that we ignore as they occur around us. It is crucial that we recognize these events, even if years after the fact; we are here to learn, after all.

I look down at the floor and again see the bear, the trout and the moose. They are stationary, yet seem to know their place; they are noble, yet static.

Tomorrow, someone else may buy the same style of rug I chose, and take it to their cabin. They will hopefully sit down with a cup of coffee, look at the lake, and reflect on the importance of the simple lessons in their lives.

The Bear, the Trout,
and the Moose

I

The Lake

The Bear

Ursus americanus

"Yogi" and "Boo Boo" formed my earliest perception of bears. They were lazy, fun-loving creatures with the next meal in mind. "Boo Boo" had some semblance of a conscience, but "Yogi" was just plain mischievous.

I have never seen a bear in the wild, although I have traveled to Grand Marais, Minnesota and hiked, with my daughter, up this hill around the north shore of Lake Superior. "Don't feed the bears" we were told. I was anticipating "Yogi" and "Boo Boo" with every step, napkins around their necks, awaiting a "pic-i-nick basket."

My more immediate concern was that their cousins were going to be a bit less courteous and even less selective of their next meal.

We think of stuffed bears as a child's toy, full of warmth and cuddliness. In reality, bears probably don't like to be hugged. They are opportunists and survivors, threatened by man and misunderstood in their pursuit of their next meal. They have adapted to their environment, and probably just want to live and let live.

If only we could learn something from the bears.

1

The Trout

Oncorhynchus mykiss

Bears eat trout.

Men eat trout.

Occasionally, men eat bears, and yes, bears have been known to eat men.

If you fall from your boat, and are not found for several days, I suspect the trout would eat you; the moose would likely look upon this scene with total indifference.

This is a strange relationship, but nature seems to enjoy the irony.

I, however, prefer my place in the food chain.

The Moose

Alces alces

I previously mentioned my foray to Grand Marais, Minnesota. My sons and I flew there one weekend, while my wife and daughter drove there earlier in the week.

We went to a restaurant called the "Pie Place," and were standing at the cashier's counter, when a man (or woman, I'm not sure) dressed as a moose entered the restaurant. He/she gave away candy, because they were celebrating "Moose Madness" in Grand Marais that weekend. This is as close as I have been to a moose, real or unreal.

Moose (Mooses?) seem like solitary creatures. They don't bother bears or trout that I have ever heard. They have been known to charge a man, but I suspect that is because he had wandered into their domain. I have heard that people eat moose meat; after all, they do look like cattle.

We celebrate the moose on our rugs. They clean our feet, and we walk on them.

They have a special place in our lives; they live with bears and trout.

I say, let them live.

A Half-Frozen Lake

(Reprinted by Permission of South Dakota State Medical Association, © 2006)

I wrote this story early one Sunday morning, in a dimly lit kitchen, over my coffee at our cabin on Lake Madison. My wife is constantly reminding me that just because I am awake, it doesn't mean the whole world wants to be awake.

I remember floating over the partially frozen lake. Looking down, I could see the control stick in my right hand, throttle in my left hand, and snowmobile boots on the rudder pedals. It gets quite cold in South Dakota in February, especially in an airplane made of tube and fabric; the "heater" was for moral support only.

I looked out over the lake and could see geese in open water beginning to take flight as I must have disturbed their morning solitude. It was odd to see open water, no less geese so early in the year.

The 1943 Taylorcraft L-2, with its sixty-five horsepower Continental engine, more floated than flew. The North-South runway at the Madison airport came into view. I reduced power and made a straight-in landing, ending a most pleasant flight.

I taxied up to the parking area, closed the throttle, and cut the "mags" to shut off the engine. I exited as gracefully as possible from the tandem cockpit, wearing a bulky snowmobile suit.

It was 1977, and I was just beginning my flying adventures as my log book would attest. Many more aircraft would follow the Taylorcraft, culminating in my current 1958 Cessna 310. The engines are up to 480 horsepower; the heater is more than adequate. Entrance and egress from the cockpit are also much more graceful.

4

Oh, I know that I must have a "thing" for older aircraft, but I find it reassuring in a world of constant change, that it is still possible to appreciate the marvels around us that have inherent time-proven attributes: durability, trustworthiness and stability.

The world of medicine is a lot like the world of aviation. It offers us the opportunity to meet people who are rich in similar time-proven attributes: patience, honesty, and acceptance. Our busy schedules do not often afford adequate time to appreciate these qualities, but they are often still there, right in front of us.

We go into medicine to treat the sick but are also given the opportunity to explore relationships with humanity in all conditions of life, health and infirmity; age doesn't automatically mean "beyond useful life."

Medicine can be like another day of flying—floating over a half-frozen lake, looking at the geese, and listening to the hum of the engine, all the while adding another entry into the log book.

Sandstorm

Images, like a mirage, come into view as you stare at the dawn.

The endless caravan stopped at the oasis, as it had for centuries; water is forever precious and a sign of safety and rest. The hiatus had been anticipated by all, as the journey was long and monotonous. Five thousand, ten thousand or possibly fifteen thousand. It was hard to tell.

Many mysteries surrounded their movement:

How did they navigate in such an endless sea of white?

Who gave the command for them to leave?

Who gave the order to stop?

Especially puzzling, was, who were those darkly clad stragglers near the rim of the encampment? They appeared to be disciples, not yet worthy, separated from the main group.

Then, it happened:

A staccato of gunfire from a well-planned attack. Within seconds the camp was responding to the ambush. A sandstorm erupted in all directions. Their voices were a flurry of curses in a foreign tongue.

The attackers moved quickly now, retrieved the unfortunate, and then slipped away.

The travelers reassembled, minus their fallen comrades, and continued their trek.

I walked away from the window, poured myself another cup of coffee, and watched the snow-geese depart.

II

The Farm

Cottonwood Trees

I have faced many obstacles in my life. I reflect back on tasks from my youth for strength and direction. My father taught me to tackle the toughest of jobs with determination, and to never even entertain defeat.

When God finished the Rocky Mountains and the Black Hills, he must have decided to make a living object of similar durability; thus, he made cottonwood trees. Cottonwood trees have been known to withstand wind, flood, locust, fire and most other curses from the Old Testament.

We had a giant cottonwood tree growing in our backyard when I was a youth. It had miraculously died, as its roots had been devoured by a swineherd (they're there in the Old Testament too, as I recall).

The point is, it needed to come down, or so my father told me. When you are fifteen years old and growing up on a farm in South Dakota, and your father says a tree must come down, you take it personally. I was given a bucksaw to accomplish the task.

I had never seen such a tool in my lifetime. A bucksaw is a giant piece of steel, four feet long and ten inches wide with ragged teeth and a wooden handle on one end. It looked to me like a prehistoric alligator's jaw. It was the perfect object of intimidation, given the nature of the project.

How could any earthly creation withstand such a challenge?

I began my first lesson in humility, ending after only thirty minutes, with calluses the size of bloated wood ticks on the palms of my hands.

The next day, I brought an ax. The calluses only grew in size, but the cottonwood tree was obviously made of some otherworldly material. I then tried fire until my father intervened; it's hard to hide smoke.

Two weeks later, my father had a neighbor who owned a combination bulldozer and backhoe come in and dig as deep as he could into the roots of the tree. He had me (of course) climb as high as I could into the tree and attach a steel cable around the trunk. The steel cable was attached to the end of a single-axle Ford bulk truck, filled with 16,000 pounds of Golden Sun cattle supplement. Our faithful "A" John Deere tractor and loader was attached to the front of the bulk truck via a polypropylene tow rope (a verrry thick, polypropylene tow rope) with oversized hooks on each end.

I took a perch on the top of the barn (my usual station when I wanted to see some really interesting developments on the farm). My father was on the tractor and my older brother was in the bulk truck.

The moment of truth arrived when my father and brother drove their vehicles forward, straining the rope and cable respectively; the bulldozer was used to push as high up the tree as it could reach with its front blade.

What happened next seems to this day as though it occurred in a dream. The tree began to fall, but our calculations were off. The top of the tree caught the power lines that reached from the 1940s era "REA" pole to the adjacent granary. The wires did not break, but instead the REA pole snapped at its base and shot forward like in a medieval movie where a castle is under siege and being pelted with giant arrows. Fortunately, the "arrow" went under my brother's truck. The wires, however, draped across the metal cable between the tree and his truck.

I froze, as I watched the events unfold. My brother had the peace of mind to jump from the truck onto the ground without touching both truck and ground. My father similarly departed the tractor.

The defiant tree lay still on the ground.

No one said a word.

I crawled down from the top of the barn.

We called the "REA" repairmen, who asked us several times how we managed to create such chaos from this simple task. They put in a new pole that stands to this day.

My brother and I don't talk about this event very often, unless we are trying to put our father in a very foul mood.

I am not entirely sure what I learned that day, but I certainly have acquired a lot more respect for cottonwood trees.

The Blacksmith

I had the distinct pleasure of growing up when small towns still had a blacksmith. These were fiercely independent men with broad shoulders and leathery hands, who made it their business to work with steel, iron and fire.

Our blacksmith shop had a certain smell and feel. The smell was of dirt and grease and the feel was crude with an earthy power.

You could always tell when the blacksmith was behind in his work, for the farmers would be standing over his work. This did not please our local blacksmith at all, and the projects would thus take most of the day.

I always seemed to have good luck with the blacksmith in getting my project done before anyone else's. I would walk into the shop with my broken piece of equipment, lay it at my feet and say nothing. Eventually the blacksmith would flip his mask up, walk over and drawl, "Whall, Richard, what have you got this time?" I would explain what had broken, but always ended it with the phrase, "and I don't know if it can be fixed."

This was the ultimate challenge, apparently, as the blacksmith would then say, "Whall, why don't you just go over to the café for 'bout an hour, then come on back."

I would come back in forty-five minutes and the piece would be finished, lying on the ground, warm to the touch.

I would thank him, take the piece, write a check and go back to work.

The blacksmith would then flip his mask down and return to his work.

No Pig Left Behind

The United States Marine Corps has a saying: "No man left be-
hind." I did not realize that it also applied to farm animals.

I had come home from high school one fall afternoon, and
was greeted by my father. He had decided to go to the local
sale barn, fifty miles away, and see if there were any
half-grown pigs for sale, as corn was cheap. He had bought
a single pig early in the sale, hoping to purchase more as the
sale continued. Apparently, other half-grown pigs had de-
cided to stay home that day.

My father loaded the single pig into his small truck,
drove home, backed up to the loading chute, opened the
back door, but no pig was inside. He informed me that we
needed to retrace his fifty miles to the sale barn and retrieve
this escape artist.

I have never been one to shy away from adventure, so
off we went.

We scanned the ditches between our farm and the
town, but no pig. We arrived at the sale barn, inquired at the
office, but no pig. We were frustrated by now, and decided
an "A &W" root beer would be appropriate.

We had driven less than two miles from town, when
my father's right arm shot in front of my face, "There he is!"

Our truck slid to a stop next to the highway; my root
beer went flying. There in the ditch, next to a driveway, lay a
half-grown pig.

We both jumped from the truck, expecting the pig to
meekly await our rescue, but he bolted for an adjacent field.

My father and I chased the renegade pig for nearly an
hour. Back and forth we went across the prairie grass, the
pig never closer than ten yards from us.

He finally ran across a road and into a farmyard. He

11

found his way into an open garage where we were able to corner and tackle him. I ran back nearly a mile to retrieve the truck. We devised a cover for the truck box to deter any more feats of swine acrobatics.

We drove the half-grown pig home, where he survived and lived out his last few months consuming cheap corn.

III
Trial and Error

The Colt

I learned to fly when I was nineteen years old, more on a whim, than by plan. It's funny how early decisions tend to follow you through your life.

The air was turbulent for October, but such days are not unusual if you fly in South Dakota. The PA-22-108, or "Piper Colt" was at the mercy of the thermals, but we were able to maintain altitude and heading with some degree of respect.

I had tentatively purchased the airplane from a man my age in Nebraska, with the agreement that he fly it to my home airport in South Dakota, with me as his passenger. He would then be given a bus ticket home, as busses still were a reasonable form of transportation in the 1970s.

I was a bit nervous, having made the deal to purchase the airplane without informing my parents. The combination of turbulence and trepidation resulted in my sleeping on the trip home. This was enough of a distraction to the pilot, that he made his final approach to the unfamiliar airport at a higher than normal rate of speed.

We landed "hot and long" and continued our rollout on the runway, approaching the intersection of the adjacent runway at about fifty miles per hour. I turned my head to the left to tell him to slow down if he wanted to make the upcoming intersection, when something to the right caught my eye. Another airplane had landed at the intersecting runway, and was approaching us at a similar rate of speed, no more than 200 feet from where I was sitting. He must have seen it too, because rather than applying the brakes, he opened the throttle on the Colt to try to get airborne and out of their way.

We became airborne just as their left wing smashed into the Colt's fuselage, about three feet behind my head. We continued our upward momentum, but with the fuselage severed, and tail structure dragging behind like a wounded bird, the Colt began to fall to earth, nose first.

We hit the ground at a forty-five-degree angle, flipped over, and came to a grinding halt. We hung suspended by our seatbelts. In a moment of great clarity, we unhooked the seatbelts, fell to the roof of the plane and scrambled out onto the runway. Gasoline was pouring out of the wing-tank fillers. The bent propeller was lying ten feet away in the form of a wry smile (or frown, if viewed upside down). The passengers in the other airplane were fortunately, unhurt. Our injuries were limited to bruised forearms, personal frustration and shame.

The airplane we had been riding in was essentially destroyed, except for the passenger cabin. I do not know why it did not burn. The other airplane had its left wing shortened by four feet and had substantial propeller damage from the ground strike.

The call to my parents required a great deal of salesmanship to first inform them that I was purchasing an airplane, and then to inform them that it was lying in a twisted heap in the middle of the airport. The ride home with my father was rather silent.

I realize now that I had cheated death that day. The Colt had bucked me off.

Bullet

I have never understood the personality of a horse, but I think they have me completely figured out.

My first memories of riding a horse were of a Shetland pony named "King." He was barrel-chested, and had the disposition of a Hereford steer: wanting to be fed, but not ridden.

My subsequent forays into horsemanship were similarly cursed. My sister Diana, on the other hand, had the balance and "oneness of spirit" it takes to ride with ease. She could bring a horse from the pasture in the Spring, apply the bridle and saddle, and take off with caution and confidence.

Bullet was a horse of many talents. He lived in our pasture over the winter months, grazed at will, harassed the cattle, yet could be caught and ridden by my sister with minimal effort. This was a very difficult scenario for my ego, but would prove at least as challenging as the "Colt" that had nearly ended my life earlier.

Diana brought Bullet out of the pasture late that Spring, applied the bridle and saddle, and cautiously rode him around the farm. She asked me if I wanted to ride. Being older than her, I took this as a personal challenge. She did remind me, in all fairness, that Bullet was a very perceptive horse, who could smell fear and lack of horsemanship; I was unmoved.

I got into the saddle and trotted in the ditch for about a quarter of a mile to the west of our farm, turned Bullet toward home, and muttered the fateful phrase, "Giddy-up."

The next few moments of my life were a blur. The horse took off on a dead run. I was hanging on for dear life, my legs squeezing his sides. Each thunderous step was amplified by the sensation that I was tilting to the right; the cinch on the saddle was coming loose, and I was leaning toward a combination woven wire and barbed wire fence.

The moment of truth came when my center of gravity overcame my grip, and I fell off the right side of the horse to the ground; I missed the fence by the grace of God.

I know for a fact it was a dry year in South Dakota, and we had but one mud puddle on the whole farm; it became my landing zone.

I fell on my back, sent muddy water flying in all directions, nearly drowning myself. I would have been all right, except for the dirty insult, had it not been for his right rear hoof planting firmly into the center of my chest. I had never before been stepped on by a horse on a dead run, but felt that this was my "final roundup."

I rolled out of the puddle, covered from head to toe with mud. I could not breathe, as my wind had been knocked from me. It took a full twenty to thirty seconds before I could speak. The first word I spoke was unrepeatable, followed by numerous adjectives, coloring my initial impression.

My mother, sister and a farm employee came running up, convinced that I was dying.

I was placed in a car and driven at a high rate of speed to the hospital. Five miles down the road, I convinced them to return me to the farm, as I did not want to have to explain "this" episode to our family doctor.

I missed three weeks of baseball that Summer, as I found it impossible to bat or throw a ball with a hoof print in the middle of my bruised chest.

It was becoming clear to me that horses, or for that matter, aircraft named after horses should be avoided, in the future, at all cost.

IV

Rhymes and Reasons

I wrote this poem on an airline napkin, about thirty minutes out of Minneapolis, on our flight home from a church-mission trip to Nicaragua.

Nicaragua

Whenever I awake to the sounds of the morn',
I will think of you, Nicaragua.

Whenever I see a school bus go by,
I will think of you, Nicaragua.

Whenever I see a crowded street,
I will think of you, Nicaragua.

Whenever I see children, laughing and playing,
I will think of you, Nicaragua.

Whenever I hear songs, sung with joy,
I will think of you, Nicaragua.

Whenever I have more than I need to eat,
I will think of you, Nicaragua.

Whenever I feel that love and hope are gone,
I will think of you, Nicaragua.

Whenever I wish, I were gone for a day,
I will think of you, Nicaragua.

I used to walk aimlessly through our pastures in the Spring, marveling at the flowing water from melting snow and Spring rains. I knew they would be there for only a few days, but what fun those few days were.

Unmapped River

The mighty Nile is on the map.
And Missouri flows without a map,

And changes maps with lines it draws
Twain state and state and country broad.

But a river is hidden in April pastures.
I've seen the torrents of thawing blizzards

That die as dawn blasts forth its heat.
Springtime rays reveal the least

Of hiding places, like amber grass.
And bleached out skeletons that breathed their last

The same October that killed the grass;
Awakened now. But the bones, alas,

Will lend their marrow, which is washed on,
As unchecked water now bursts from ponds

That hold no more. And soon my river
Will blast and boil and start to quiver

The earth around, though now concealed.
Where are the map makers? Not in my field.

Who hasn't looked forward to the end of the week?

Laid Back Friday

Laid back Friday, brings me down.
Ain't nobody in this town.

There's a ringing in my brain,
Like the echo, of a passing train

That bends the tracks, and makes them squeak.
When iron on iron, grinds its teeth.

No decisions are made today.
However it falls, fall it may.

What a waste of precious time,
Funny though, I feel just fine.

The Black Hills of South Dakota hold some of the most unexpected surprises in a state 250 miles wide and 400 miles long, where only 750,000 people reside.

Request

Larger requests, I'm sure have been made,
But I'd like to borrow your hills for a day.

To feel the rush of a trout-filled stream,
Would fly me to heaven, on a rainbow's beam.

To smell a campfire as it smolders and smokes
In a curling, conical, sky-filling soak.

To hear the rustle of leaves in the wind,
Or a tumbling creek near my tent, is no sin.

To taste the air with the sweetness of morn';
For a day, I request to be happy and warm.

To see up to heaven, through boughs of green,
And never look back on a happier scene.

Larger requests, I'm sure have been made,
But none so rewarding, as this perfect day.

Sometimes it's fun just to play with words, and see where they land.

Shadows

Shadows dance upon the wall.
Some are thin, some are tall.

With nothing there, they void the light
And cast it back, without a fight.

A shadow can wear a smile or frown,
A true facsimile of up and down

That never rests, as on the earth
They faithfully travel, with frequent mirth.

You'll never see a tardy shadow,
For they can move like zinging arrows

That find their mark, without an err',
As they remain the message bearers

Of light, removed from backstage walls,
And rainbows hanging from waterfalls.

Yes! Rainbows have a shadow too,
However fine against the blue.

A shadow lives where light outlines
The world we see, the hills and pines

That void the light, and cast the dark
Upon the earth: Behold their mark.

I moved from the farm to the city at twenty-three years old, where the Summer nights were much more frantic than I had been used to. This poem seemed to summarize what I was seeing and feeling at that time.

Full Moon

Under the spell of another full moon,
The city is tense, like a bride in June.

Lightning is flashing, with distant thunder,
The storms to the west are poised to plunder.

The air is heavy like a sweat-soaked shirt,
Tomorrow's mud will be yesterday's dirt.

Bars are filled, and glasses are empty,
The mood is alive, as no one has plenty.

The band is playing a C.W. tune,
And parking lot fights will be hopping soon.

Four lanes of traffic, two going each way,
Teenagers in hot rods are out to play.

Ice cream nights, and swimming pool days,
Full moon's power is here to stay.

Softball games carry into the night,
The crowd's unruliness: the umpire's plight.

Police sirens scream as they chase down offenders,
Ambulances wail as they tend fender benders.

The lake reflects the stare of the moon,
Like a one-eyed sailor who peers through the gloom

And scans the horizon, to find his way home,
Past rocks and wrecks, and white-capped foam.

Under the spell of another full moon,
The city never sleeps; she's just out of tune.

Knowing that not all tasks are done by Summer's end.

A Stretch of Summer

More than just a lazy dawn.
Thicker than a weed-filled lawn.

This heat-filled air that sticks to the skin,
Is everywhere, like rust on tin.

The Summer seems to fry my spirit
Beyond well done; Ninety degrees or near it.

The month of June's a memory.
Hello, July. What is you fee?

A field of corn. Is that enough?
Or, do you wish, some other stuff?

Some wheat for lunch? A lake to sip?
Leave some for August, to wet her lips

For she'll be here, throughout the last
Of Summer's stretch, to guard her catch,

Of finished fields, and dying grass.
We'll toast the Summer, from a half-filled glass.

27

I am always telling my children: "Focus on the task, not the emotion." I believe we see things more clearly at night, when we are not distracted by all the "emotions" of the day.

Night Life

When the sun decides to sail away,
And the work is done for another day.

I find a spot beneath the trees,
To just lie back and feel the breeze.

The sky is clear, with the air crisp tonight,
The farmhouse windows stare into the night.

The stars are still, as they hang in the sky,
Their images, reflected by the pond's cool tide.

A million thoughts try to enter my mind,
But I cast them aside, as I start to unwind.

I yell at the dog to "stop chasing the cats,"
Who've begun their prowling for mice or young rats.

I live for these moments, when I see for myself,
That the background so scenic, is truly a wealth.

It's there in the daylight, too simple to see,
Revealed in the twilight, just waiting for me.

When your day is over, take a break, and delight
In the simple solutions, right there in the night.

Summer ends abruptly in South Dakota, with all the grace of an avalanche.

Winter's Race

I'd like to say a thing or two,
Before the frost replaces the dew.

I do not like the fact that Fall
Is so impatient to make its call

And end the Summer, although July
Was here and gone; boy did it fly.

The morning chill that hits my face,
Awakens me to the coming race

Of leaves to die, and flowers to bow
Their heads to Winter. And tell me how

The Summer can leave, why, yesterday
Seemed like the first, or second of May.

But, somewhere in my haste to taste
The sweetness of Summer, I let it waste

Away, and pass. And now I face
The cold reality of Winter's race,

That I must run through ice and snow,
'Till Spring returns and lets me know

That leaves must die that trees might grow.
So, let us welcome, the coming snow.

Old friends can always recall your best stories.

The Trail

We leave a trail wherever we go,
Not just in the Winter, when squashing the snow.

The people we meet in our daily lives,
Are told all our stories, our truths and our lies.

We're touching each other with glances and phrases,
And leaving impressions, like burning grass blazing.

We bring joy with favor, and pain when we hate,
Like ink on white paper, it's hard to erase.

So, start your day early, and say what you mean,
The trail there behind you will be wide and clean.

Author David Laskin wrote in "The Children's Blizzard" of the terrible hardships endured by the people living on the prairie during the blizzard of 1888. My great-grandfather was the Danish immigrant John Jensen he referred to, who lost his wife and two daughters in the storm. He then remarried, and his first son became my grandfather. Many children died, because the storm hit at noon, after they had gone to school on a mild, January morning.

The Children of '88

Voices of children, muffled by snow.
Cries for Mothers, to let them know

That they'd be fast asleep in the cold.
They'd gone to school as they'd been told.

The morning light could not foretell,
That they'd been sent into a hell

Of cold and wind and breathless swells.
Of piling snow, where many fell.

The storm hit fast, at noon or so.
The teachers said that they must go

To find their homes. So row on row
The children marched in headlong snow.

The younger ones could not keep up.
The older ones told them just

To hold on tight, and with some luck
They'd all be home before the dusk.

A few did find their way back home.
But many more lay down, as shown

By scores and scores of tiny forms
They found there in the morning cold.

Do not forget the way they cried.
Do not forget the way they died.

Do not forget that we're alive,
Because of those who did survive.

Hush, now, go to sleep.

Hush, now, go to sleep.

Hush now, it's too late.

For the children of '88.

V

On the Road

Rueben

Some of my fondest memories center around my travels to the Rosebud Indian Reservation.

I traveled between Sioux Falls and Mission, SD to the Rosebud Indian Reservation for two years, doing an outreach clinic at the Rosebud Hospital. I left an old car at the Mission, SD airport, and would fly in to the airport, driving the old car the last ten miles of the journey.

Mission is a very remote town, and Rosebud is even more remote. The Mission airport had one runway, pointing up-hill to the northwest and down-hill to the southeast. It had no office, telephone or toilet facilities. It did, however, have an old trailer home, where a man named Henry lived.

Henry was a very simple man, and had a dog named "Rueben."

Rueben was a mongrel, and did not like pilots, doctors or any other strangers who might think they could use his runway. He would hide under the trailer house until you approached within about ten yards, and then ambush you. I liked Rueben anyway, but he never let me pet him.

The Mission airport was slated for runway improvement one Summer, and the heavy construction vehicles were scattered around the field. I landed one hot Summer day, and walked over to the trailer house to say hello to Henry, but no Rueben.

Henry came out, so I asked him where Rueben was. It turned out that Rueben liked to sleep under the large trucks, and had gotten run over when a vehicle had started and backed up, without his awakening first.

I told Henry how sorry I was that Rueben had died, and suggested he could always get a puppy to replace him. Henry pointed to his chest, scarred from a recent bypass surgery, and said: "That would hurt too much here."

I continued my flights to Mission, but soon, Henry was gone also. It would be easy to explain that his heart disease had simply progressed. I really think, though, that his heart just could not take any more "hurt."

A Holy Place

People go on "mission trips" with their church all the time. The goal is to help people in need and learn about their culture. If you are lucky, you may encounter the real world you are visiting.

It was our second full day in Nicaragua. We had just finished our third clinic, and were requested to drive a few blocks out of our way to see an old woman who was too ill to come to see us. We got in the bus, and drove the few blocks to the bottom of a hill. Several of us got out, and used a flashlight to safely climb the hill to her home.

We found a small wooden building at the top of the hill, with a man waiting outside to greet us. We entered the building and found an old woman lying on a simple bed made from two boards. A colorful blanket covered her body, and a scarf covered her head. We said hello and offered to examine her. It did not take long to determine that she was dying of end-stage liver disease. She looked more than ninety years old, but informed us that she was fifty-three.

Her voice was amazingly strong, and she said that she had little pain. She also told us that she possessed more than all the riches of the world, because she had Christ.

One of our group suggested we take a picture before we left, so I volunteered. I looked around the room to get the best perspective for the picture, when it suddenly struck me, that we were standing in a stable. I looked through the viewfinder, and there at the top of the picture, above the woman, was a picture of Christ, attached to the wall.

I took the photograph, but as we left I realized that we had indeed been invited to visit a holy place.

Horsepower

I guess horses aren't so bad after all.

The ride to the country airport, eight miles from my home, takes no more than ten minutes. I pass by droves of commuters traveling toward the city, away from my destination.

I am the first pilot to arrive at 6:45 A.M. I sense the solitude of slumbering aircraft, but I am certain they note my interruption. I choose my steed from the hangar, inspect her airframe and start her engines. Headset on, taxi to the starting gate, run-up her engines to make sure she is ready, turn into the wind and apply power: Giddy-up!

The adjacent highway is 200 yards to my left and merging slowly with the angle of the runway. A Mustang on a dead run comes into my peripheral vision, challenging me at this early hour. I pull away steadily. Gear up at 90 knots. Climb at 110 knots; the Mustang loses by a furlong.

We contact departure as we climb to 6,000 feet. The flight plan has been opened and I am passed on to Minneapolis Center. Course 232 degrees. Airspeed 173 knots.

I look back at the earth and the commuters are moving at a crawl. The Missouri River is low this time of year, and I am able to cross safely.

Forty miles in the distance, the rural Nebraska airport comes into view.

Whoa!!

We enter the pattern, land and taxi to the airport ramp. I shut down the engines, greet the airport manager and order "oats" for the ride home. I hop into a "courtesy car," ride two miles to town; the dew on the windows does not have time to clear.

I enter the hospital, leave my things at the nurse's station, walk to the dialysis unit, greet the nurses and patients and start my rounds.

The Mustang is likely only halfway to Sioux City by now.

I have seen things today few people can even imagine, and my day has just begun. I sincerely hope the rest of the trail is as fulfilling.

VI

Final Assessment

A Moment in Time

My father and I were returning to Sioux Falls from Winner, SD, when he mentioned that he had found his grand-mother's gravesite just north of Highway 44, near the town of Ola. The site was rather remote, and was the smaller of two cemeteries, just a few miles south of Chamberlain, on the east side of the Missouri River. He had inquired in town about the cemeteries, and had found her gravesite at the smaller one.

He said he had found the marking stone tipped over near the back of the cemetery, and had worked to chip away the frozen ground and set the stone back upright, in a re-spectable fashion. He could not remember the exact direc-tions to the site, except that it was further from town than the larger cemetery, and less elaborate.

A couple of months later, I was in Chamberlain at the dialysis unit. I had recently acquired a patient from that area. When he informed me he was from Ola, a town no lon-ger on many maps, my curiosity piqued. I asked him about the cemeteries near Ola, and he informed me that there in-deed are two cemeteries nearby—the larger one where the Scandinavians were buried, and the smaller German one, which is less accessible. He doubted that the smaller one was the one I was looking for, given my Scandinavian ancestry. He gave me the directions to the smaller cemetery anyway, and I committed them to memory.

The next time I was in Chamberlain, I found that I had a couple of extra hours between patients, so I set off to find the site. I drove the exact directions, 15 miles in all, and found myself on a township road with scarcely enough gravel to cover the dirt beneath. It was cold, dreary and drizzly, near the end of March. I looked in both directions at the intersection of a dirt path that crossed the road, and saw a small stand of trees off to my left, about 100 yards from the road. I put the Jeep into 4-wheel drive, drove down the dirt path, and could clearly see a cemetery coming into view. I slipped and skidded around, but managed to pull up onto some higher ground away from the mud.

As I walked up to the cemetery, a strange loneliness overcame me. The names, apparently from several families, were all unfamiliar to me.

I walked back, as if by instinct, to a secluded corner of the cemetery, away from the main group, and there saw a gray marking stone, about two feet high. I walked around to its face and saw the name "Bertha Heggen." A short verse had been inscribed onto the face, but was now unreadable. The date of her death was March 15, 1904.

I could clearly visualize a gathering of immigrants dressed in black, standing on the cold, barren prairie, saying goodbye to Bertha. The wind muffled their prayers. Their horse-drawn wagons were nearby. I especially felt the presence of a five-year-old girl standing with her family, wondering where her mother had gone, and why everyone was crying. I could see them walking away, and someone picking up young Nellie and carrying her as they left for the wagons.

That young girl would have nine children and have to put two of them back into the earth, as babies, before her passing. Her fourth child would be my father. I am certain that such thoughts were far from her mind on that cold and dreary day.

I reached out to the stone, laid my hand upon it, and touched the past.

Solace

It's OK to slow down, even when you are traveling at the speed of light.

My mind pictures canoes at the bend of a river, campfire lit with smoke rising lazily upward, and a well-lit tent with flaps open, welcoming the tired traveler.

I enter the scene near the shore of the river, and walk over crackling kindling and giant boulders, deposited when glaciers departed the area. I can smell the coffee and taste the stew.

I am a doctor today, 170 miles from home. My clinic is slower today, because the first snow of the season is threatening to arrive. My airplane is home in its hangar, at a small country airport; I didn't mind the drive today at all.

Medicine is changing in front of my eyes, with falling reimbursement and more government oversight. Every generation of retiring doctors tells the next to "not go into medicine anymore;" obviously, it is too late for me.

I am going to sit back today, enjoy my patients and my coffee, and return to my mind's world, where I belong.

Banana Popsicles

My brother and I used to think that a few coins in the palm were the greatest treasure of all.

Two cents for a twelve-ounce bottle. Five cents for a quart bottle: Colas, 7-UP, Orange soda. All the bottles we can find and carry; run to the grocery store, two blocks away.

Count them out, get the coins; just enough for two popsicles.

Root beer?—banana? Root beer?—banana? Root beer?—banana?

Banana today!

—Maybe root beer tomorrow.

Fried Fish for Supper

My mother's parents were Greek immigrants who never learned to drive, but loved their simple life together.

I don't remember my grandfather working, but I remember buying minnows with him. The visions are timeless: They are for sale across the street at "Charley's" house, in a garage in the back. You have to walk past a concrete bird bath, with broken glass shards embedded on its surface.

Bamboo poles for my brother and I, but an open-faced rod and reel for my grandfather.

We walk with him, down to the Third Street Bridge. Set up our lines, but try not to fall in. We are fishing next to the spillway, and no one who falls in ever comes back up to the surface, even after they drown.

How come the bullheads are so easy for me to catch, and the crappies so elusive? I am so bored, after just as few minutes.

Grandpa always ends up with a stringer full of crappies.

We walk home, uphill, all the way.

A stringer of fish he shows off to my grandmother. She lays them into a dishpan under the faucet in the basement, and fills the pan with water; the smell is distinct.

Let them soak for now.

Fried fish for supper.

He's Lost His Marbles

The brain is a complex organ, holding our memories and realities in a glass case.

My father was placed in the dementia unit of a nursing home, following his brother's death over a year ago. They had been life-long business partners, and his brother's death had apparently been more than he could handle.

My father lapsed into a coma a week after my uncle's funeral, but awoke several weeks later in an apparent state of chronic dementia; there seemed to be no hope.

I would visit my father in the nursing home regularly, but he seemed to only vaguely recognize me. He would smile upon my entrance, and then drift back into the clouds.

I had been, coincidentally, following a patient from his boyhood community with an acute kidney ailment. She could not drive—her husband had died several years earlier—and she was being driven to my clinic, alternately, by her neighbors.

One of the designated drivers turned out to be the widow of one of my father's childhood friends. She waited until the end of her neighbor's visit, stood up, and presented me with a faded blue and white marble.

She told me that her husband and my father had been best of friends growing up, exploring old barns and winding creeks for any sign of adventure. One day, my father had apparently told her husband that if they would plant some marbles in the earth, they would grow, providing them with an endless supply.

Years later, a pheasant hunter had been walking in that field, found a lone marble at his feet, showed it to her husband, who related the story to the hunter. Her husband had kept the marble, a sign of his boyhood days, until his death; she handed me the marble and I took it home.

I brought the marble along to my next nursing home visit, handed it to my father, and tried to relate the story. My father, surprisingly, launched into a story of his boyhood adventures with his deceased friend. They would apparently wander the farmland around their homes, climbing so high inside old barns that they could scarcely find their way down. He said that he was surprised they had even survived their childhood; he even recounted his friend's death.

My father continued to improve markedly after that, and recently was able to be discharged from the nursing home. No one seems to know how he lapsed into this state of apparent dementia, nor how he recovered.

I think, however, that he just needed to "find his marbles."

Have you ever stopped, felt the wind, and realized that we're not going to be around forever? Did you ever wonder if that's OK?

There's No Such Thing As Wasted Time

We do not own the day.
We do not own the night.
The seconds, minutes and hours
Will pass from left to right.

Our arrival is not needed.
Our presence will not last.
The time we're here, from beat to beat
Can slip away so fast.

Our lives should not be measured,
By what we do each day.
There's no such thing as wasted time:
There's nothing more to say.

A little music at the end of the day: priceless!

Twilight Moods

Another dark enlightened room
Awaits me at the twilight's tune.
Another album weaves its tales,
As I sit back and let my sails catch every breeze that blows
    my way.

And though I've wandered, I yearn to stay
In twilight moods;
This finished day has followed me here:
So let it stay.

Target: "Ainsworth"

Isolated Midwestern and prairie towns swelled during World War II, as they became training sites for the fighter and bomber crews, training for risky missions over France and Germany. Many of these airports still carry signs of a larger purpose.

The drive from Sioux Falls, South Dakota to Ainsworth, Nebraska, takes three hours and forty minutes. It is a journey through rolling hills and a treeless landscape. The halfway point is Wagner, SD, on the Yankton Sioux Indian Reservation.

The flight from Tea (yes, there is actually a town named "Tea" in South Dakota), or Lincoln County Airport takes just under one hour. Not surprisingly, Wagner again becomes the halfway point, but from there the flight takes on a mystical property.

Ten miles of flight beyond Wagner brings you to the bleached banks and shores of the Missouri River, where the "sand-hills" of Nebraska ultimately take on their rough and rolling character. There is an absence of landmarks, except for the town of Butte, Nebraska, between the contrasts of the gentle farmland around Wagner, and the hilly landscape leading to the Ainsworth Airport.

The final beacon becomes the Niobrara River, whose course is that of a flattened "V." The right hand arm of the V is perfectly in line with the airport, more than forty miles away, but reassures what your GPS indicates: you are on the correct flight path.

The airport is about eight miles west of town, and comes into view like some expansive mirage. There are two runways, each over one mile long, that arise from the local terrain; the taxiways seem to go on forever.

The airport was used, during World War II, to train

fighter pilots and bomber crews for the Army Air Corps. An oversized hangar still graces the west side of the field; the B-17's, P-39's and P-47's are gone.

I wonder how many boys and young men looked down at these gentle rolling hills, only to be later transported to the skies over France and Germany. The Niobrara and Missouri Rivers became the Rhine and Danube. The bleached banks of the Missouri became the white cliffs of Dover. White puffs of a building overcast became black puffs of deadly flack. A distant flight of geese turned into a swarm of ME-109's, setting up their next "kill."

Landing at the airport in an older twin-engine airplane only reinforces the feeling that you have stepped through some sort of time portal.

I depart my aircraft, chock the nose wheel, and am ready to relay the results of my "mission" to anyone who might want to ask. No one is around at this early hour, except the wind, and the voices from the past.

I hop into the airport car (I was anticipating an army Jeep), and head for town.

I'm back on friendly soil.

Mission accomplished.

Party Line

My mother lived on the farm, as a fish out of water. She made the best of being a city girl on an isolated prairie farm.

My mother's parents moved to South Dakota from Greece. She was born in Redfield, SD and grew up in Huron, SD. Our farm was twenty miles from Huron, a city of more than 10,000 and four miles from Alpena, SD, a town of about 300.

Our means of communication was via "dry-cell" telephones. These were a large wooden box, mounted on the wall, with a crank on the side and bells on top to alert you who was calling whom. Our phone number was "53," but we were "A long and three shorts" on the ringer.

You always knew who was being called, by listening to the number of long and short rings. If you really needed to know what was going on, you quite simply lifted the receiver, and listened in.

My mother would call her mother in Huron, almost daily, to lament the life on the farm. She would also use the opportunity to "gossip" about the neighbor ladies. The only problem, she would start the conversation in English, and then convert to Greek, after stating the neighbor's name. The neighbor women became so infuriated, that they got together with my mother, and explained the function and benefits of a "party line."

A party line was a way for farm wives to discuss what bothered them about their neighbors, without confronting them directly. Problems were identified, and the people identified were politely made aware of their deficiencies. Behaviors changed, and life went on.

A few years later, our wooden-box phone was replaced by a "pink" (the hot color in kitchens in 1963) rotary phone. The party line went away, and so did one of the best group therapy modalities on the prairie.

Brownian Movement

Brownian Movement: The random movement of particles in fluid.

Random molecules of DNA form Denmark and Norway come together in South Dakota in 1926. Random molecules of DNA from the Greek Islands come together in South Dakota in 1928. Further random molecules of DNA come together in a random moment of affection on November, 1953 on the plains of South Dakota.

Fifty-four years later, sitting in front of a random computer, random molecules of ink are deposited on a random sheet of paper, formed from random molecules of cellulose; the book goes on a random shelf.

A random book is chosen from a random bookstore, and a random thought is transmitted to random neurons on a random cruise in the Greek Islands, in the bustle of Denmark, on the fjords of Norway or the plains of South Dakota; the movement is continuous.

René Descartes said: *"Cogito, ergo sum:* I think, therefore I am."

Hmmm.

I think, therefore I am—*Lucky!*